A CELTIC

David Adam was born in Alnwick, Northumberland, and until his recent retirement he was vicar of Holy Island. He was the vicar of Danby in North Yorkshire for over twenty years, where he discovered a gift for composing prayers in the Celtic pattern. His first book of these, *The Edge of Glory*, achieved immediate popularity, and he has since published several collections of prayers and meditations based on the Celtic tradition. His books have been translated into various languages, including Finnish and German, and have appeared in American editions.

A Celtic Psaltery

Compiled by David Adam

Published in Great Britain in 2001 by
Society for Promoting Christian Knowledge
Holy Trinity Church
Marylebone Road
London NW1 4DU

British Library Cataloguing-in-Publication Data

A catalogue record for this book is available from the British Library

ISBN 0–281–05218-2

Typeset by Wilmaset Ltd, Birkenhead, Wirral
Printed and bound in Great Britain by
Bookmarque Ltd, Croydon, Surrey

Contents

Introduction

There is a book of songs that has been in use for three thousand years: they are songs of grief and glory. About half way in its lifetime the song book was brought to Ireland and the other Celtic lands and immediately they fell in love with it. As books were scarce, most of those who loved the songs learnt them off by heart. From memory they sang them, or recited them every day, and sometimes seven times a day a group joined together to say them. Because they were committed to memory, even when they were travelling they still sang or said their songs. It must have been quite impressive to have met a group like those who travelled with St Aidan and to hear their chanting:

> His life is in marked contrast to the apathy of our own times, for all who walked with him, whether monks or layfolk, were required to meditate, that is, either to read the scriptures or to learn the Psalms. This was their daily occupation where ever they went.
>
> (Bede, *A History of the English Church and People*, Book 3, ch. 5)

The songs were the Book of Psalms from the Old Testament. They were learnt not by rote but by devotion; it was not so much a matter of the mind as of the heart. If you were to take part in daily worship it was necessary to know the psalms off by heart, especially Psalm 119 as it would be said every day! In fact, some young monks were known to have asked if you could say Psalm 119 twelve times a day instead of saying all the psalms: no doubt they had learnt the longest psalm by common use and not the rest of the Psalter. We learn that at the monastery of Tallaght in the ninth century they sometimes said the *Beati* (Psalm 119) twelve times instead of saying the whole Psalter. Also from Tallaght we hear of an enquiry whether it would be allowed to recite only 50 psalms a day with instruction rather than the whole Psalter without instruction. However, Maelruain of Tallaght said he did not think saying the whole Psalter daily too much of a task to be made lighter by shortening it. Whatever a brother's work, he was expected to stop for the daily offices and the recitation of the Psalms, the 'three fifties' as they were often called. Maelruain added:

The monk who labours with the sickle or the flail, who works with the sledgehammer, and who digs a trench, each has to chant the three fifties in addition to his daily labour, and none of them eats an evening meal until he has finished all of them.

Here is a comment from the Rule of Tallaght on how the Psalms were said.

'I have heard', said Mael Dithruib, 'that Dublitir's manner of performing the vigil was to recite the Psalter (three fifties) standing and with a genuflection at the end of each psalm.'

'This is not my way of carrying it out,' said Maelruian. 'I chant every alternate fifty psalms standing or sitting in turn. Anyone who remained seated for a longer period would fall asleep, someone who remained standing for all the psalms would be exhausted.'

The Psalms are full of all the joys and sorrows of life and if you look there is a psalm for every situation. Above all the Psalms were used to express a deep love for God and a trust in him. Like many of the church people of their times, the Celtic peoples were devoted to the Psalter. There is an early poem where a monk speaks of his mistress with whom he had slept: he tells of how others had slept with her after they had parted. He calls her Crinog, 'the old one who is ever young' or 'the young old one'.

TO CRINOG

Crinog, melodious is your song,
Though young no more you are still bashful.
We two grew up together in Niall's northern land,
When we use to sleep together in tranquil slumber.

That was my age when you slept with me,
O peerless lady of pleasant wisdom:
A pure-hearted youth, lovely without a flaw,
A gentle boy of seven sweet years.

We lived in the great world of Banva
Without sullying soul or body,
My flashing eye full of love for you,
Like a poor innocent untempted by evil.

Your just counsel is ever ready,
Wherever we are we seek it:
To love your penetrating wisdom is better
Than glib discourse with a king.

Since then you have slept with four men after me,
Without folly or falling away:
I know, I hear it on all sides,
You are pure without sin from man.

At last, after weary wanderings
You have come to me again,
Darkness of age has settled on your face:
Sinless your life draws near its end.

You are still dear to me, faultless one,
You shall have welcome from me without stint:
You will not let us be drowned in torment;
We will earnestly practise devotion with you.

The lasting world is full of your fame,
Far and wide you have wandered on every track:
If every day we followed your ways,
We should come safe into the presence of dread God.

You leave an example and a bequest
To everyone in this world,
You have taught us by your life;
Earnest prayer to God is no fallacy.

Then may God grant us peace and happiness!
May the countenance of the King
Shine brightly upon us
When we leave behind us our withered bodies.

(Meyer, 1928, pp. 37–8)

There is a nice thrill in reading about a monk with his mistress, and if you read carefully he was with her from the age of seven! A young lad was allowed to join a monastic community and its school of learning from the age of seven; it was there he met her. Over the passing years four others had the use of her, but in her old age and a little tattered she somehow found her way back to one who truly loved her. This mistress is the Psalter. His pride in the Psalter is expressed in the words:

> Your just counsel is ever ready,
> Wherever we are we seek it:
> To love your penetrating wisdom is better
> Than glib discourse with a king.
>
> (Meyer, 1928, p. 37)

It is said of Egbert who travelled from England to Ireland and went to the monastery of Rathmelsigi that he would recite the entire Psalter every day to the praise of God and in thanksgiving for escaping the plague.

There is no doubt that words learnt in devotion and recited every day would deeply influence the mind and the thought-patterns of all who did this. It is not surprising that in every age they would also seek to produce new songs that applied to their situation. Sometime they would try and make them deliberately like the Psalter. 'The Saltair Na Rann' or 'The Psalter of Verses', also known as 'The Celtic Psalter', is the longest poem from early Ireland. This poem is purposely divided into 150 parts in imitation of the Psalms from the Old Testament. However, the contents of the Celtic Psalter related the Bible story from the creation in Genesis through to the resurrection of Christ. The Saltair Na Rann is attributed to Oengus the Ceile De, an Irish hermit of the ninth century, though it is now thought that the Saltair is most likely from the tenth century. The first of the 'psalms' in this book are from the Saltair Na Rann.

When you read the *Confession* of St Patrick you realize how well he knew his Scriptures and there is a feeling of the rhythm of the Psalms in his writing. In section two and three of the *Confession* it sounds very like the Psalter.

> The Lord revealed to me the sense of my unbelief,
> that I might remember my sins, that I might turn to Him with my whole heart.
> God looked upon my lowliness: and had pity on the ignorance of my youth.
> He cared for me before I knew Him:
> before I had gained wisdom to separate good from evil.
> As a father comforts his son, He protected me.
> It is only right and proper to tell of His many blessings:
> to tell of the grace the Lord gave me in the land of my captivity.
> I tell you all these things to return thanks to my God.

After being corrected I came to an awareness of God.
O that we might glorify Him and bear witness to His wonderful
works.

(trans. David Adam)

The oldest known writing from Ireland is on wax tablets dating
from about the year AD 600 and this is from the Book of Psalms.
These well-preserved tablets were found in the Springmount Bog
in County Antrim and they contain Psalms 30–32. They were
probably used to instruct students.

The next oldest writing, and the oldest Irish manuscript, is also
of the Psalms and is from the sixth to the seventh century. This
was a whole psalter and represents a very pure form of St Jerome's
translation of the Psalms; it is known as the 'Psalter of St
Columba' or 'the Cathach (The Battler) of St Columba'. It is
attributed to Columba of Iona and could well have been written in
his own hand. This psalter has lost some pages and now has only
Psalm 30.10 to Psalm 105.13 (Vulgate numbering).

The deep love for psalms gave a feeling for verse and a desire to
express one's love for God in every situation. There were songs
for guidance and songs for protection; there were hymns for the
morning and others for the evening. It became natural to pray to
God and to praise him in every situation. Sometimes praise would
be alone and at other times part of the daily ritual of an ordinary
village community. Such an approach to worship has left us with a
wealth of material that has enriched the world and work of
believers. What better way to proclaim God's presence than to be
able to talk freely to him at all times? (Though this was always
only for those who had eyes and ears to understand.) What better
way to keep in touch with God than to turn our hearts and voices
to him at regular points during the day?

There is much we can learn from the songs and poems of the
Celtic peoples. The selection I have chosen are ones I have been
able to use to enrich my own private worship, or as part of a
service for a group of people.

CREATION

The heavens declare the glory of God: and the firmament sheweth his handiwork.

(Psalm 19.1)

O come, let us sing unto the Lord: let us heartily rejoice in the strength of our salvation.
Let us come before his presence with thanksgiving:
and shew ourselves glad in him with psalms.

(Psalm 95.1–2)

IN THE BEGINNING

My King, my own King, King of the heavens,
without pride and without any opposition,
You created the whole world,
eternal and ever victorious King.

King above the elements, higher than the sun:
King greater than the ocean's depths,
King in the South and North, in the East and West,
King against whom no one can triumph.

King of the mysteries, you were and are
before the elements, before all ages,
King without beginning, without end,
King eternal, beautiful to behold.

King, you created the shining heaven
yet, you are not over-bearing or over-powering.
You created the world full of delight
making it strong, powerful and stable.

King, you fashioned the great deep
out of the primary stuff of the elements,
shaping its wondrous formless mass.
King, you formed out of it each element,
You made them without any restriction,
a beautiful mystery, tempestuous, yet serene,
the animate and the inanimate.

(trans. David Adam)

THE SHAPING OF THE EARTH

King, you shaped with glory, with energy,
out of the malleable primal stuff,
the great and weighty round earth,
its foundations, its height, its length, its breadth.

King, you shaped without narrow limits
in the circle of the sky,
the round sphere of the earth,
like a good apple perfect and sound.

King, after that, you shaped and set
the new matter of the earth,
the smooth current of the cold and watery air,
above the world forever flowing.

King, you filtered the cold splendid water,
from the great mass of splendid mountains,
shaping it into streams, and rivers,
and great reservoirs of water,
each according to their measure and moderation.

(trans. David Adam)

THE CREATION OF THE WINDS

King, you ordained the eight winds,
Each moving with sureness and full of beauty:
the four primary winds you harness,
and the four fierce under-winds.
There are four lesser under-winds,
as the learned writers say,
this makes the numbers of the winds,
without error or doubt, to twelve in all.

King, you gave the colours to each wind
and set them in their courses,
each in their own individual manner,
their own ordered disposition,
each having a variety of colour:

The white wind, the clear purple,
the blue, and the powerful green,
the yellow and red, gentle winds without anger.

The black, the grey, the speckled,
the dark, the deep brown and the dun
all dark coloured winds,
not light nor easily controlled.

King, you ordered over every space,
the eight wild under-winds,
and you laid down without fault or error
the boundaries of the four primary winds.

From the east the smiling purple,
From the south the pure and wondrous white,
From the north the blustering and moaning black,
From the west the rippling and babbling dun wind.

The red and yellow
the white and the purple,
the green and the brave blue,
the dun and the pure white.

The grey and the dark brown, hated for harshness,
the dun and the deep black:
the dark speckled easterly wind,
both black and purple.

All truly ordered in their shapes
their natures were ordained,
with wise restraints
according to their fixed position and place.

The twelve winds,
Easterly, Westerly, Northerly, Southerly,
The King, who harnesses them, holds them in place,
He fettered them with seven restraints.

O King, who gave to them according to their position
around the world with so many restraints,
a single harness around each two winds
and one restraint for them all.
O King, you arranged them in beautiful harmony,
each one according to their ways within their limits,
at one time they would be peaceful in filling the space
and at another time they would be tempestuous.

                                        (trans. David Adam)

GOD OF ALL

Our God is the God of all,
The God of heaven and earth,
Of the sea and of the rivers;
The God of the sun and of the moon and of all the stars;
The God of the lofty mountains
and of the lowly valleys.
He has His dwelling around heaven and earth,
and sea, and all that in them is.
He inspires all,
He gives life to all,
He dominates all,
He supports all.
He lights the light of the sun.
He furnishes the light of the night.
He has made springs in dry land . . .
He is the God of heaven and earth,
of sea and rivers,
of sun, moon and stars,
of the lofty mountain and the lowly valley,
the God above heaven,
and in heaven,
and under heaven.

(St Patrick)

THE LORD OF CREATION

Let us adore the Lord,
Maker of marvellous works,
Bright heaven with its angels,
And on earth the white-waved sea.

Old Irish

(Davies and Bowie, 1995, p. 30)

GLORIFICAMUS TE

I offer Thee
Every flower that ever grew,
Every bird that ever flew,
Every wind that ever blew,
　Good God!

Every thunder rolling,
Every church bell tolling,
Every leaf and sod!
　Laudamus Te!

I offer Thee
Every wave that ever moved,
Every heart that ever loved,
Thee, my Father's Well-Beloved.
　Dear Lord.

Every river dashing,
Every lightning flashing,
Like the angel's sword.
　Benedicimus Te!

I offer Thee
Every cloud that ever swept
O'er the skies and broke and wept
In rain, and with the flowerlets slept.
　My King.

Each communicant praying,
Every angel staying
Before Thy throne to sing.
　Adoramus Te!

I offer Thee
Every flake of virgin snow,
Every spring of earth below,
Every human joy and woe,
　My Love!

O Lord! And all the glorious
Self o'er death victorious,
Throned in heaven above.
    Glorificamus Te!

                    Ancient Irish
                (translator unknown)

HAIL GLORIOUS LORD!

Hail, all glorious Lord! with holy mirth
May Church and chancel bless Thy good counsel!
Each chancel and church,
All plains and mountains,
All ye three fountains –
Two above wind,
And one above earth!
May light and darkness bless Thee!
Fine silk, green forest confess Thee!
Thus did Abraham father
Of faith with joy possess Thee.
Bird and bee-song bless Thee,
Among the lilies and the roses!
All the old, all the young
Laud Thee with joyful tongue,
As Thy praise was once sung
By Aaron and Moses.
Male and female,
The days that are seven,
The stars of the heaven,
The air and the ether,
Every book and fair letter;
Fish in waters fair-flowing,
And song and deed glowing!
Gray sand and green sward
Make you blessing's award!
And all such as with good
Have satisfied stood!
While my own mouth shall bless thee
And my Saviour confess Thee.
Hail glorious Lord!

> *Black Book of Carmarthen*, tenth–eleventh century
> (Graves, 1917, p. 75)

ST COLUMBA IN IONA

Delightful it would be
From a rock pinnacle to trace
Continually
The Ocean's face:
That I might watch the heaving waves
Of noble force
To God the Father chant their staves
Of the earth's course.
That I might mark its level strand,
To me no lone distress,
That I might hark the seas-bird's wondrous band –
Sweet source of happiness.
That I might hear the clamorous billows thunder
On the rude beach.
That by my blessed church side might I ponder
Their mighty speech.
Or watch surf-flying gulls the dark shoal follow
With joyous scream,
Or mighty ocean monsters spout and wallow,
Wonder supreme!
That I might well observe of ebb and flood
All cycles therein;
And that my mystic name might be for good
But 'Cul-ri. Erin'.
That gazing toward her on my heart might fall
A full contrition,
That I might bewail my evils all,
Though hard the addition;
That I might bless the Lord who all things orders
For their good.
The countless hierarchies through heaven's bright borders –
Land, strand and flood/
That I might search all books and from their chart
Find my soul's calm.
Now kneel before the Heaven of my heart,
Now chant a psalm;

Now meditate upon the King of heaven,
Chief of the Holy Three;
Now ply my work by no compulsion driven
What greater joy could be?
Now plucking dulse from rocky shore,
Now fishing eager on,
Now furnishing food unto famished poor;
In hermitage anon:
The guidance of the King of kings
Has been vouchsafed to me;
If I keep watch beneath His wings,
No evil shall undo me.

(Graves, 1917, pp. 20–1)

JESU WHO OUGHT TO BE PRAISED

It were as easy for Jesu
To renew the withered tree
As to wither the new
Were it His will so to do.
Jesu! Jesu! Jesu!
Jesu! meet it were to praise Him.

There is no plant in all the ground
But is full of His virtue,
There is no form in the strand
But is full of His blessing.
Jesu! Jesu! Jesu!
Jesu! meet it were to praise Him.

There is no life in the sea,
There is no creature in the river,
There is naught in the firmament,
But proclaims His goodness.
Jesu! Jesu! Jesu!
Jesu! meet it were to praise Him.

There is no bird on the wing,
There is no star in the sky,
There is nothing beneath the sun,
But proclaims His goodness.
Jesu! Jesu! Jesu!
Jesu! meet it were to praise Him.

(Carmichael, 1983, pp. 39–41)

PRAISING GOD

Let us praise God
at the beginning
and the end of time.
Who ever seeks Him out
He will not deny
not refuse.

> *Black Book of Carmarthen*, tenth–eleventh century
> (Graves, 1917, p. 75)

THE LIGHTENER OF THE STARS

Behold the Lightener of the stars
On the crests of the clouds,
And the choralists of the sky
Lauding Him.

Coming down with acclaim
From the Father above,
Harp and lyre of song
Sounding to Him.

Christ, Thou refuge of my love,
Why should I not raise Thy fame!
Angels and saints melodious
Singing to Thee.

Thou Son of the Mary of graces,
Of exceeding white purity of beauty,
Joy were it to me to be in the fields
Of Thy riches.

O Christ my beloved,
O Christ of the Holy Blood,
By day and by night
I praise Thee.

(Carmichael, 1983, p. 45)

ALMIGHTY CREATOR

Almighty Creator, it is you who have made
the land and sea . . .

The world cannot comprehend in song bright and melodious,
even though the grass and trees should sing,
all your wonders, O true Lord!

The Father created the world by a miracle;
it is difficult to express its measure.
Letters cannot contain it, letters cannot comprehend it.

Jesus created for the hosts of Christendom,
with miracles when he came,
resurrection through his nature.

He who made the wonder of the world,
will save us, has saved us.
It is not too great a toil to praise the Trinity.

Clear and high in the perfect assembly,
Let us praise above the nine grades of angels
The sublime and blessed Trinity.

Purely, humbly, in skilful verse,
I should love to give praise to the Trinity,
according to the greatness of his power.

God has required of the host in this world
who are his, that they should at times,
all together, fear the Trinity.

The one who has power, wisdom and dominion
above heaven, below heaven, completely;
it is not too great a toil to praise the Son of Mary.

Old Welsh, *c.* ninth century
(Davies and Bowie, 1995, pp. 27–8)

A HYMN OF PRAISE

Blessing and brightness,
Wisdom, and thanksgiving,
Great power and might
To the King who rules over all.

Glory and honour and goodwill,
Praise and the sublime songs of minstrels,
Overflowing love from every heart
To the King of Heaven and Earth.

To the chosen Trinity has been joined
Before all, after all, universal
Blessing and everlasting blessing,
Blessing everlasting and blessing.

(Davies and Bowie, 1995, p. 29)

PRAISE BEYOND WORDS

Almighty Creator, who hast made all things,
The world cannot express all thy glories,
Even though the grass and the trees should sing.

The Father has wrought so great a multitude of wonders
That they cannot be equalled.
No letters can contain them, no letters can express them.

He who made the wonder of the world
Will save us, has saved us.
It is not too great a toil to praise the Trinity.

Purely, humbly, in skilful verse
I should delight to give praise to the Trinity.

Old Welsh, ninth century
(trans. Ifor Williams)

MORNING

I will magnify thee, O God, my King:
and I will praise thy Name for ever and ever.
Every day will I give thanks unto thee:
and praise thy Name for ever and ever.
Great is the Lord, and marvellous worthy to be praised:
there is no end of his greatness.

Psalm 145.1–3

RUNE BEFORE PRAYER

Old people in the Isles sing this or some other short hymn before prayer. Sometimes the hymn and prayer are intoned in low, tremulous, unmeasured cadences like the moving and moaning, and soughing and sighing of the ever-murmuring sea on their own wild shores.

They generally retire to a closet, to an outhouse, to the lee of a knoll, or to the shelter of a dell, that they may not be seen or heard of men. I have known men and women of 80, 90 and 100 years of age continue the practice of their lives in going from one to two miles to the seashore to join their voices with the voicing of the waves and their praises with the praises of the ceaseless sea.

I am bending my knee
In the eye of the Father who created me,
In the eye of the Son who purchased me,
In the eye of the Spirit who cleansed me,
In friendship and affection.
Through Thine own Anointed One, O God,
Bestow upon us fullness in our need,
Love towards God,
The affection of God,
The smile of God,
The wisdom of God.
The grace of God,
The fear of God,
And the will of God
To do on the world of the Three,
As angels and saints
Do in heaven;
Each shade and light,
Each day and night,
Each time in kindness,
Give Thou us Thy Spirit.

(Carmichael, 1983, pp. 2–3)

COME I THIS DAY

Come I this day to the Father,
Come I this day to the Son,
Come I to the Holy Spirit powerful;
Come I this day with God,
Come I this day with Christ,
Come I with the Spirit of kindly balm.

God, and Spirit, and Jesus,
From the crown of my head
To the soles of my feet;
Come I with my reputation,
Come I with my testimony,
Come I to Thee, Jesu;
Jesu, shelter me.

(Carmichael, 1983, p. 69)

PRAYER AT DRESSING

My mother would be asking us to sing our morning song to God down in the back-house, as Mary's lark was singing it up in the clouds, and as Christ's mavis was singing it in yonder tree, giving glory to the God of the creatures for the repose of the night, for the light of the day, and for the joy of life. She would tell us that every creature on the earth here below and in the ocean beneath and in the air above was giving glory to the great God of the creatures and the worlds, of the virtues and of the blessings, and would we be dumb!

(Carmichael, 1976, p. 25)

Bless to me, O God,
My soul and my body;
Bless to me, O God,
My belief and my condition;

Bless to me, O God,
My heart and my speech,
And bless to me, O God,
The handling of my hand;

Strength and busyness of morning,
Habit and temper of modesty,
Force and wisdom of thought,
And Thine own path, O God of virtues,
Till I go to sleep this night;

Thine own path, O God of virtues,
Till I go to sleep this night.

(Carmichael, 1976, p. 27)

PRAYER

Thanks to Thee ever, O gentle Christ,
That Thóu hast raised me freely from the black
And from the darkness of last night
To the kindly light of this day.

Praise unto Thee, O God of all creatures,
According to each life Thou hast poured on me,
My desire, my word, my sense, my repute,
My thought, my deed, my way, my fame.

(Carmichael, 1976, p. 29)

THE DEER'S CRY

I arise today
Through a mighty strength,
the invocation of the Trinity,
Through belief in the threeness,
Through confession of the oneness
Of the Creator of Creation.

I arise today
Through the strength of Christ's birth with His baptism,
Through the strength of His crucifixion with His burial,
Through the strength of His resurrection with His ascension,
Through the strength of His descent for the judgement of Doom.

I arise today
Through the strength of the love of the Cherubim,
In obedience of angels,
In the service of archangels,
In the hope of resurrection to meet with reward,
In prayers of patriarchs,
In predictions of prophets,
In preaching of apostles,
In faith of confessors,
In innocence of holy virgins,
In deeds of righteous men.

I arise today
Through the strength of heaven:
Light of sun,
Radiance of moon,
Splendour of fire,
Speed of lightning,
Swiftness of wind,
Depth of sea,
Stability of earth,
Firmness of rock.

I arise today
Through God's strength to pilot me:
God's might to uphold me,
God's wisdom to guide me,
God's eye to look before,
God's ear to hear me,
God's word to speak for me,
God's hand to guard me,
God's way to lie before me,
God's shield to protect me,
God's host to save me
From snares of devils,
From temptation of vices,
From every one who shall wish me ill,
Afar and near,
Alone and in a multitude.

(attributed to St Patrick)

THANKSGIVING

Thanks be to Thee, O God, that I have risen today,
To the rising of this life itself;
May it be to Thine own glory, O God of every gift,
And to the glory of my soul likewise.

O great God, aid Thou my soul
With the aiding of Thine own mercy;
Even as I clothe my body with wool,
Cover Thou my soul with the shadow of Thy wing.

Help me to avoid every sin,
And the source of every sin to forsake;
And as the mist scatters on the crest of the hills,
May each ill haze clear from my soul, O God.

(Carmichael, 1976, p. 31)

A PRAYER FOR GRACE

I am bending my knee
In the eye of the Father who created me,
In the eye of the Son who died for me,
In the eye of the Spirit who cleansed me,
In love and desire.

Pour down upon us from heaven
The rich blessing of Thy forgiveness;
Thou who art uppermost in the City,
Be Thou patient with us.

Grant to us, Thou Saviour of Glory,
The fear of God, the love of God, and His affection,
And the will of God to do on earth at all times
As angels and saints do in heaven;
Each day and night give us Thy peace.
Each day and night give us Thy peace.

(Carmichael, 1983, p. 35)

PRAYER AT RISING

Bless to me, O God,
Each thing mine eye sees;
Bless to me, O God,
Each sound mine ear hears;
Bless to me, O God,
Each odour that goes to my nostrils;
Bless to me, O God,
Each taste that goes to my lips;
Each note that goes to my song,
Each ray that guides my way,
Each thing that I pursue,
Each lure that tempts my will,
The zeal that seeks my living soul,
The Three that seek my heart,
The zeal that seeks my living soul,
The Three that seek my heart.

(Carmichael, 1976, p. 33)

MORNING PRAYER

I believe, O God of all gods,
That Thou art the eternal Father of life;
I believe, O God of all gods,
That Thou art the eternal Father of love.

I believe, O God of all gods,
That Thou art the eternal Father of the saints;
I believe, O God of all gods,
That Thou art the eternal Father of each one.

I believe, O God of all gods,
That Thou art the eternal Father of mankind;
I believe, O God of all gods,
That Thou art the eternal Father of the world.

I believe, O Lord and God of the peoples,
That Thou art the creator of the high heavens,
That Thou art the creator of the skies above,
That Thou art the creator of the oceans below.

I believe, O Lord and God of the peoples,
That Thou art He Who created my soul and set its warp,
Who created my body from dust and from ashes,
Who gave my body breath, and to my soul its possession.

Father, bless to me my body,
Father, bless to me my soul,
Father, bless to me my life,
Father, bless to me my belief.

Father eternal and Lord of the peoples,
I believe that Thou hast remedied my soul in the Spirit of
    healing,
That Thou gavest Thy loved Son in covenant for me,
That Thou hast purchased my soul with the precious blood of
    Thy Son.

Father eternal and Lord of life,
I believe that Thou didst pour on me the Spirit of grace
at the bestowal of baptism

Father eternal and Lord of mankind,
Enwrap Thou my body and my soul beloved,
Safeguard me this night in the sanctuary of Thy love,
Shelter me this night in the shelter of the saints.

Thou hast brought me up from last night
To the gracious light of this day,
Great joy to provide for my soul,
And to do excelling good to me.

Thanks be to Thee, Jesu Christ,
For the many gifts Thou hast bestowed on me,
Each day and night, each sea and land,
Each weather fair, each calm, each wild.

I am giving Thee worship with my whole life,
I am giving Thee assent with my whole power,
I am giving Thee praise with my whole tongue,
I am giving Thee honour with my whole utterance.

I am giving Thee reverence with my whole understanding,
I am giving Thee offering with my whole thought,
I am giving Thee praise with my whole fervour,
I am giving Thee humility in the blood of the Lamb.

I am giving Thee love with my whole devotion,
I am giving Thee kneeling with my whole desire,
I am giving Thee love with my whole heart,
I am giving Thee affection with my whole sense;
I am giving Thee my existence with my whole mind,
I am giving Thee my soul, O God of all gods.

My thought, my deed,
My word, my will,
My understanding, my intellect,
My way, my state,

I am beseeching Thee
To keep me from ill,
To keep me from hurt,
To keep me from harm;

To keep me from mischance,
To keep me from grief,
To keep me this night,
In the nearness of Thy love.

May God shield me,
May God fill me,
May God keep me,
May God watch me.

May God bring me
To the land of peace,
To the country of the King,
To the peace of eternity.

Praise to the Father,
Praise to the Son,
Praise to the Spirit,
The Three in One.

(Carmichael, 1976, pp. 14–47)

GOD'S AID

God to enfold me,
God to surround me,
God in my speaking,
God in my thinking.

God in my sleeping,
God in my waking,
God in my watching,
God in my hoping.

God in my life,
God in my lips,
God in my soul,
God in my heart.

God in my sufficing,
God in my slumber,
God in mine ever-living soul,
God in mine eternity.
        (Carmichael, 1976, p. 53)

EVENING

I will lay me down in peace, and take my rest:
for it is thou, Lord, only, that makest me dwell in safety.

Psalm 4.9

SLEEP CONSECRATION

I am lying down tonight,
With Father, with Son,
With the Spirit of Truth,
Who shield me from harm.

I will not lie with evil,
Nor shall evil lie with me,
But I will lie down with God,
And God will lie down with me.

God and Christ and the Spirit Holy,
And the cross of the nine white angels,
Be protecting me as Three and as One,
From the top tablet of my face to the soles of my feet.

Thou King of the sun and of glory,
Thou Jesu, Son of the Virgin fragrant,
Keep Thou us from the glen of tears,
And from the house of grief and gloom,
Keep us from the glen of tears,
From the house of grief and gloom.

(Carmichael, 1983, p. 87)

GOD WITH ME LYING DOWN

God with me lying down,
God with me rising up,
God with me in each ray of light,
Nor I a ray of joy without Him,
Nor one ray without Him.

Christ with me sleeping,
Christ with me waking,
Christ with me watching,
Every day and night,
Each day and night.

God with me protecting,
The Lord with me directing,
The Spirit with me strengthening,
For ever and for evermore,
Ever and evermore, Amen.
Chief of chiefs, Amen.

> (Carmichael, 1983, p. 5)

REPOSE OF SLEEP

O God of life, darken not to me Thy light,
O God of life, close not to me Thy joy,
O God of life, shut not to me Thy door,
O God of life, refuse not to me Thy mercy,
O God of life, quench Thou to me Thy wrath,
And O God of life, crown Thou to me Thy gladness,
O God of life, crown Thou to me Thy gladness.

(Carmichael, 1976, p. 343)

A PRAYER

O God,
In my deeds,
In my words,
In my wishes,
In my reason,
And in the fulfilling of my desires,
In my sleep,
In my dreams,
In my repose,
In my thoughts,
In my heart and soul always,
May the blessed Virgin Mary,
And the promised Branch of Glory dwell.
Oh! in my heart and soul always,
May the blessed Virgin Mary,
And the fragrant Branch of Glory dwell.

(Carmichael, 1983, p. 27)

SLEEPING PRAYER

I am placing my soul and my body
On Thy sanctuary this night, O God,
On Thy sanctuary, O Jesus Christ,
On Thy sanctuary, O Spirit of perfect truth;
The Three who would defend my cause,
Nor turn Their backs upon me.

Thou, Father, who art kind and just,
Thou, Son, who didst overcome death,
Thou, Holy Spirit of power,
Be keeping me this night from harm;
The Three who would justify me
Keeping me this night and always.

(Carmichael, 1983, p. 73)

PATRICK'S EVENSONG

Christ, Thou Son of God most High,
May Thy Holy Angels keep
Watch around us as we lie
In our shining beds asleep.

Time's hid veil with truth to pierce
Let them teach our dreaming eyes,
Arch-King of the Universe,
High-Priest of the Mysteries.

May no demon of the air,
May no malice of our foes,
Evil dream or haunting care
Mar our willing prompt repose!

May our vigils hallowed be
By the tasks we undertake!
May our sleep be fresh and free,
Without let and without break.

(Graves, 1917, p. 16)

THE GIFTS OF THE THREE

Spirit, give me of Thine abundance,
Father, give me of Thy wisdom,
Son, give me in my need,
Jesus beneath the shelter of Thy shield.

I lie down tonight,
With the Triune of my strength,
With the Father, with Jesus,
With the Spirit of might.

(Carmichael, 1983, p. 75)

SMOORING THE FIRE

The sacred Three
To save,
To shield,
To surround
The hearth,
The house,
The household,
This eve,
This night,
Oh! this eve,
This night,
And every night,
Each single night.
Amen.

   (Carmichael, 1983, p. 235)

PROTECTION

Whoso dwelleth under the defence of the Most High:
shall abide under the shadow of the Almighty.
I will say unto the Lord, Thou art my hope, and my strong hold:
my God, in him will I trust.

Psalm 91.1–2

THE PROTECTION OF CHRIST

Christ as a light
Illumine and guide me!
Christ as a shield overshadow and cover me!
Christ be under me! Christ be over me!
Christ be beside me,
On left hand and right!
Christ be before me, behind me, about me!
Christ, this day, be within and without me!

(St Patrick)

THE PROTECTING GOD

Lord, be with us this day,
Within us to purify us;
Above us to draw us up;
Beneath us to sustain us;
Before us to lead us;
Behind us to restrain us;
Around us to protect us.

(St Patrick)

PRAYER OF ST COLUMBA

Have mercy, Christ, have mercy
on all that trust in Thee,
for Thou art God in glory
to all eternity.

O God, make speed to save us
In life's abounding throes:
O God, make haste to help us
In all our weary woes.

O God, Thou art the Father
of all that have believed:
from whom all hosts of angels
Have life and power received.

O God, Thou art the Maker
of all created things,
the righteous Judge of judges,
the Almighty King of kings.

High in the heavenly Zion
Thou reignest God adored;
and in the coming glory
Thou shalt be sovereign Lord.

Beyond our ken Thou shinest,
The everlasting Light;
ineffable in loving,
unthinkable in might.

Thou to the meek and lowly
Thy secrets dost unfold;
O God, Thou doest all things,
all things both new and old.

I walk secure and blessed
in every clime or coast,
in the Name of God the Father,
and Son, and Holy Ghost.

(attributed to Columba
trans. Duncan Macgregor)

COLUMBA'S AFFIRMATION

Alone with none but Thee, my God,
I journey on my way;
What need I fear, when Thou art near,
O King of night and day?
More safe I am within Thy hand,
than if a host did round me stand.

My destined time is fixed by Thee,
and death doth know his hour.
Did warriors strong around me throng,
they could not stay his power;
no walls of stone can man defend
when Thou Thy messenger dost send.

My life I yield to Thy decree,
and bow to Thy control
in peaceful calm, for from Thine arm
no power can wrest my soul.
Could earthly omens e'er appal
A man that heeds the heavenly call!

The child of God can fear no ill,
His chosen dread no foe;
we leave our fate with Thee and wait
Thy bidding when we go.
'Tis not from chance our comfort springs,
Thou art our trust, O King of kings.

St Columba
(trans. unknown)

NOLI PATER

Father, do not allow thunder and lightning,
lest we be shattered by its fear and fire.

We fear you, the terrible one, believing there is none like you.
All songs praise you throughout the hosts of angels.

Let the summits of heaven, too, praise you with roaming
   lightning,
O most loving Jesus, O righteous King of kings.

Blessed forever, ruling in right government,
is John before the Lord, till now, in his mother's womb,
filled with the grace of God in place of wine or strong drink.

Elizabeth of Zechariah begot a great man:
John the Baptist, the forerunner of the Lord.

The flame of God's love dwells in my heart
as a jewel of gold is placed in a silver dish.

(Clancy and Márkus, 1995, p. 85)

ALEXANDER'S BREASTPLATE

On the face of the world
There was not born
His equal.
Three-person God,
Trinity's only Son,
Gentle and strong.
Son of the Godhead,
Son of humanity,
Only Son of wonder.
The Son of God is a refuge,
Mary's Son a blessed sanctuary,
A noble child was seen.
Great his splendour,
Great Lord and God,
In the place of glory.
From the line of Adam
And Abraham
We were born.
From David's line,
The fulfilment of prophecy,
The host was born again.
By his word he saved the blind and deaf,
From all suffering,
The ragged
Foolish sinners,
And those of impure mind.
Let us rise up
To meet the Trinity,
Following our salvation.
Christ's cross is bright,
A shining breastplate
Against all harm,
Against all our enemies may it be strong:
The place of protection.

(Davies and Bowie, 1995, p. 44)

O HELPER OF WORKERS

O helper of workers,
ruler of all good,
guard on the ramparts
and defender of the faithful,
who lift up the lowly
and crush the proud,
ruler of the faithful,
enemy of the impenitent,
judge of all judges,
who punish those who err,
pure life of the living,
light and Father of lights
shining with great light,
denying to none of the hopeful
your strength and help,
I beg that me, a little man
trembling and most wretched,
rowing through the infinite storm of this age,
Christ may draw after Him to the lofty
most beautiful haven of life
. . . an unending
holy hymn forever.
From the envy of enemies you lead me
into the joy of paradise.
Through you, Christ Jesus,
who live and reign . . .

(attributed to St Columba
Clancy and Márkus, 1995, p. 73)

THE THREE

In the name of Father,
In the name of Son,
In the name of Spirit,
Three in One:

Father cherish me,
Son cherish me,
Spirit cherish me,
Three all-kindly.

God make me holy,
Christ make me holy,
Spirit make me holy,
Three all-holy.

Three aid my hope,
Three aid my love,
Three aid mine eye,
And my knee from stumbling,
My knee from stumbling.

(Carmichael, 1976, p. 63)

CONSECRATION

How great the tale, that there should be,
In God's Son's heart, a place for me!
That on a sinner's lips like mine,
The cross of Jesus Christ should shine!

Christ Jesus, bend me to Thy will,
My feet to urge, my griefs to still;
That even my flesh and blood may be
A temple sanctified to Thee.

No rest, no calm, my soul may win,
Because my body craves to sin,
Till Thou, dear Lord, Thyself impart
Peace to my head, light to my heart.

May consecration come from far,
Soft shining like the evening star!
My toilsome path make plain to me,
Until I come to rest in Thee.

  attributed to Muredach Albanach, end of twelfth century
           (Hull, 1913, p. 156)

DEUS MEUS

Deus meus adiuva me,
Give me thy love, O Christ I pray,
Give me thy love, O Christ I pray,
Deus meus adiuva me.

In meum cor ut sanum sit,
Pour, loving King, Thy love in it,
Pour, loving King, Thy love in it,
In meum cor ut sanum sit.

Domine, da ut peto a te,
O, pure bright sun, give, give, me today,
O, pure bright sun, give, give, me today,
Domine, da ut peto a te.

Hanc spero rem et quaero quam,
Thy love to have where'er I am,
Thy love to have where'er I am,
Hanc spero rem et quaero quam.

Tuum amorem sicut uis,
Give to me swiftly, strongly, this,
Give to me swiftly, strongly, this,
Tuum amorem sicut uis.

Quaero, postulo, peto a te,
That I in heaven, dear Christ, may stay,
That I in heaven, dear Christ, may stay,
Quaero, postulo, peto a te.

Domine, Domine, exaudi me,
Fill my soul, Lord, with Thy love's ray,
Fill my soul, Lord, with Thy love's ray,
Deus meus adiuva me,
Deus meus adiuva me.

> attributed to Maelisu, eleventh century
> (trans. George Sigerson in Hull, 1913, pp. 140–1)

THE SOUL PLAINT

O Jesu! tonight,
Thou Shepherd of the poor,
Thou sinless person
Who didst suffer full sore,
By ban of the wicked,
And wast crucified.

Save me from evil,
Save me from harm,
Save Thou my body,
Sanctify me tonight,
O Jesu! tonight,
Nor leave me.

Endow me with strength,
Thou Herdsman of might,
Guide me aright,
Guide me in Thy strength,
O Jesu! in Thy strength
Preserve me.

(Carmichael, 1983, p. 71)

PRAYER FOR PROTECTION

As Thou art the Shepherd over the flock
Tend Thou us to the cot and fold,
Sain us beneath Thine own glorious mantle;
Thou Shield of protection, guard us for ever.

Be Thou a hard triumphant glave
To shield us securely from wicked hell,
From the fiends and from the stieve snell gullies,
And from the lurid smoke of the abyss.

Be my soul in the trustance of the High King,
Be Michael the powerful meeting my soul.

(Carmichael, 1983, p. 37)

THE GUARDIAN ANGEL

Thou angel of God who has charge of me
From the dear Father of mercifulness,
The shepherding kind of the fold of the saints
To make round about me this night.

Drive from me every temptation and danger,
Surround me on the sea of unrighteousness,
And in the narrows, crooks, and straits,
Keep thou my coracle, keep it always.

Be thou a bright flame before me,
Be thou a guiding star above me,
Be thou a smooth path below me,
And be a kindly shepherd behind me,
Today, tonight, and for ever.

I am tired and I a stranger,
Lead thou me to the land of angels;
For me it is time to go home
To the court of Christ, to the peace of heaven.

(Carmichael, 1983, p. 49)

CALLING UPON GOD

*Out of the deep have I called unto thee, O Lord: Lord, hear my
    voice.*
O let thine ears consider well: the voice of my complaint.

Psalm 130.1–2

A GENERAL SUPPLICATION

God, listen to my prayer,
Bend to me Thine ear,
Let my supplications and my prayers
Ascend to Thee upwards.
Come, Thou King of Glory,
To protect me down,
Thou King of life and mercy
With the aid of the Lamb,
Thou Son of Mary Virgin
To protect me with power,
Thou Son of the lovely Mary
Of purest fairest beauty.

(Carmichael, 1983, p. 13)

LORD HAVE MERCY

God above us,
God before us,
God rules.
May the King of Heaven
give now the portion of mercy.

Black Book of Carmarthen, tenth–eleventh century

(Graves, 1917, p. 75)

PETITION

Be Thou a smooth way before me,
Be Thou a guiding star above me,
Be Thou a keen eye behind me,
This day, this night, for ever.

I am weary, and I forlorn,
Lead Thou me to the land of the angels;
Methinks it were time I went for a space
To the court of Christ, to the peace of heaven;

If only Thou, O God of life,
Be at peace with me, be my support,
Be to me as a star, be to me as a helm,
From my lying down in peace to my rising anew.

(Carmichael, 1976, p. 171)

GOD BE WITH US

God be with us
On this Thy day,
  Amen.

God be with us
On this Thy night,
  Amen.

To us and with us,
On this Thy day,
  Amen.

To us and with us,
On this Thy night,
  Amen.

It is clear to be seen of us,
Since we came into the world,
That we have deserved Thy wrath,
  Amen.

Thine own wrath,
Thou God of all,
  Amen.

Grant us forgiveness,
  Amen.

Grant us forgiveness,
  Amen.

Grant to us Thine own forgiveness,
Thou merciful God of all,
  Amen.

Anything that is evil to us,
Or that may witness against us

Where we shall longest be,
Illume it to us,
Obscure it to us,
Banish it from us,
Root it out of our hearts,
Ever, evermore, everlastingly.
Ever, evermore, everlastingly.
   Amen.
      (Carmichael, 1983, pp. 15–17)

MAELISU'S HYMN TO THE HOLY SPIRIT

O Holy Spirit, hasten to us!
Move round about us, in us, through us!
All our deadened souls' desires
Inflame anew with heavenly fires!

Yea! let each heart become a hostel
Of Thy bright Presence Pentecostal,
Whose power from pestilence and slaughter
Shall shield us still by land and water.

From bosom sins, seducing devils,
From hell with its hundred evils,
For Jesus' only sake and merit,
Preserve us, Thou Almighty Spirit!

(Graves, 1917, p. 50)

HOSPITALITY

Whether my house be dark or bright,
I close it not on any wight,
Lest Thou, hereafter, King of stars
Against me close the heavenly bars.

If from a guest who shares Thy board,
The dearest dainty thou shalt hoard,
'Tis not that guest, O doubt not it,
But Mary's Son shall do without it.

(Graves, 1917, p. 338)

THE SEA-GOING BARK

Shall I loose my dusky little coracle
On the glorious, deep, wide-bosomed ocean?
Shall I face, O Heaven's bright King and Oracle,
Of my own free will the salt commotion?

Whether narrow in Thy sight or wide it be,
Served by a few or a host in number,
O my God, wilt Thou Thyself beside it be,
When my struggling bark the billows cumber.

(Graves, 1917, p. 338)

TIME FOR REPENTANCE

The time is ripe and I repent
every trespass, O my Lord.
Pardon me every crime,
Christ, as Thou art merciful.

By Thine incarnation sweet,
by Thy birth, my sacred King,
by thy lasting baptism here,
pardon me of every wrong.

By Thy hanging, filled with love,
by Thy rising from the dead,
all my passions pardon me,
Lord who art truly merciful.

By Thy ascension – glorious hour –
to holy Heaven, to the Father
(promised ere Thou didst depart)
pardon me my evil-doing.

By Thy coming – holy word –
to judge the hosts of Adam's seed,
by Heaven's orders nine revealed,
be my offences forgiven me.

By the ranks of prophets true,
by the martyrs' worthy throng,
by the train of noble Fathers,
pardon the crimes that mastered me.

By the band of pure apostles,
by the chaste disciples' host,
by each saint of royal favour,
pardon me my evil deeds.

By the great world's pious virgins,
by the prime lay-womanhood,
by Mary, Maiden wonderful,
pardon me my earthly crimes.

By Earth's peoples (sweet the word)
and those of bright and blessed Heaven
grant Thy pardon excellent
for all my crimes, since I repent!

> attributed to Oengus the Ceile De, late tenth century
>
> (trans. anonymous)

INVOCATION OF THE GRACES

A shade art thou in the heat,
A shelter art thou in the cold,
Eyes art thou to the blind,
A staff art thou to the pilgrim,
An island art thou at sea,
A fortress art thou on land,
A well art thou in the desert,
Health art thou to the ailing.

(Carmichael, 1983, p. 9)

CONSECRATION

Like as the hart desireth the water-brooks:
so longeth my soul after thee, O God.
My soul is athirst for God, yea, even for the living God:
when shall I come to appear before the presence of God?
                                        Psalm 42.1–2

JESU, THOU SON OF MARY

Jesu, Thou Son of Mary,
Have mercy upon us,
    Amen.

Jesu, Thou Son of Mary,
Make peace with us,
    Amen.

Oh, with us and for us
Where we shall longest be,
    Amen.

Be about the morning of our course,
Be about the closing of our life,
    Amen.

Be at the dawning of our life,
And oh! at the dark'ning of our day,
    Amen.

Be for us and with us,
Merciful God of all,
    Amen.

Consecrate us
Condition and lot,
Thou King of kings,
Thou God of all,
    Amen.

Consecrate us
Rights and means,
Thou King of kings,
Thou God of all,
    Amen.

Consecrate us
Heart and body,
Thou King of kings,
Thou God of all,
  Amen.

Each heart and body,
Each day to Thyself,
Each night accordingly,
Thou King of kings,
Thou God of all,
  Amen.
  (Carmichael, 1983, pp. 19–21)

DEDICATION

'Tis God's will I would do,
My own will I would rein;
Would give to God his due,
From my own due refrain;
God's path I would pursue,
My own path would disdain.

(McLean, 1961, p. 59)

FAITH AND WORKS

The tempest howl, the storms dismay,
But manly strength can win the day.
Heave lads, and let the echoes ring.

For clouds and squalls will soon pass on,
And victory lie with work well done.
Heave lads and let the echo ring . . .

The king of virtues vowed a prize
For him who wins, for him who tries.
Think lads, of Christ and echo him.

(Ó Fiaich, 1974)

PRAYER

O God, hearken to my prayer,
Let my earnest petition come to Thee,
For I know that Thou art hearing me
As surely as though I saw it with mine eyes.

I am placing a lock upon my heart,
I am placing a lock upon my thoughts,
I am placing a lock upon my lips
And double-knitting them.

Aught that is amiss for my soul
In the pulsing of my death,
Mayest Thou, O God, sweep it from me
And mayest Thou shield me in the blood of Thy love.

Let no thought come to my heart,
Let no sound come to my ear,
Let no temptation come to mine eye,
Let no fragrance come to my nose,

Let no fancy come to my mind,
Let no ruffle come to my spirit,
That is hurtful to my poor body this night,
No ill for my soul at the hour of my death;

Buy mayest Thou Thyself, O God of life,
Be at my breast, be at my back,
Thou to me as a star, Thou to me as a guide,
From my life's beginning to my life's closing.

(Carmichael, 1976, p. 71)

THE DEDICATION

Thanks to Thee, God,
Who brought'st me from yesterday
To the beginning of today,
Everlasting joy
To earn for my soul
With good intent.
And for every gift of peace
Thou bestowest on me,
My thoughts, my words,
My deeds, my desires
I dedicate to Thee.
I supplicate Thee,
I beseech Thee,
To keep me from offence,
And to shield me tonight,
For the sake of Thy wounds
With Thine offering of grace.

(Carmichael, 1983, p. 99)

DEDICATION

Rule this heart of mine,
O dread God of the elements,
That Thou mayest be my love,
That I may do Thy will.
(Meyer, 1928, p. 36)

THOUGHTS

God's will would I do,
My own will bridle;

God's due would I give,
My own due yield;

God's path would I travel,
My own path refuse;

Christ's death would I ponder,
My own death remember;

Christ's agony would I meditate,
My love to God make warmer;

Christ's cross would I carry,
My own cross forget;

Repentance of sin would I make,
Early repentance choose;

A bridle to my tongue I would put,
A bridle on my thoughts I would keep;

God's judgement would I judge,
My own judgement guard;

Christ's redemption would I seize,
My own ransom work;

The love of Christ would I feel,
My own love know.

                    (Carmichael, 1976, p. 51)

GLORY

O God, thou art my God:
early will I seek thee.
My soul thirsteth for thee, my flesh also longeth after thee:
in a barren and dry land where no water is.
Thus have I looked for thee in holiness:
that I might behold thy power and glory.

Psalm 63.1–3

HOLY FATHER OF GLORY

Thanks be to Thee, Holy Father of glory,
Father kind, ever-loving, ever-powerful,
Because of all the abundance, favour, and deliverance
That Thou bestowest upon us in our need.
Whatever providence befalls us as Thy children,
In our portion, in our lot, in our path,
Give to us with it the rich gifts of Thine hand
And the joyous blessing of Thy mouth.

We are guilty and polluted, O God,
In spirit, in heart, and in flesh,
In thought, in word, in act,
We are hard in Thy sight in sin.
Put Thou forth to us the power of Thy love,
Be Thou leaping over the mountains of our transgressions,
And wash us in the true blood of conciliation,
Like the down of the mountains, like the lily of the lake.

In the steep common path of our calling,
Be it easy or uneasy to our flesh,
Be it bright or dark for us to follow,
Thine own perfect guidance be upon us.
Be Thou a shield to us from the wiles of the deceiver,
From the arch-destroyer with his arrows pursuing us,
And in each secret thought our minds get to weave,
Be Thou Thyself on our helm and at our sheet.

Though dogs and thieves would reive us from the fold,
Be Thou the valiant Shepherd of glory near us.
Whatever matter or cause or propensity
That would bring to us grief, or pains, or wounds,
Or that would bear witness against us at the last,
On the other side of the great river of dark shadows,
Oh! do Thou obscure it from our eyes,
And from our hearts drive it for ever.

Now to the Father who created each creature,
Now to the Son who paid ransom for His people,
Now to the Holy Spirit, Comforter of might:
Shield and sain us from every wound;
Be about the beginning and end of our race,
Be giving us to sing in glory,
In peace, in rest, in reconciliation,
Where no tear shall be shed, where death comes no more.
Where no tear shall be shed, where death comes no more.

(Carmichael, 1983, pp. 23–5)

GUIDANCE

I will lift up mine eyes unto the hills:
from whence cometh my help.
My help cometh even from the Lord:
who hath made heaven and earth.
Psalm 121.1–2

BE THOU MY VISION

Be Thou my Vision, O Lord of my heart:
Naught is all else to me, save that Thou art,
Thou my best thought, by day and by night,
Waking or sleeping, Thy presence my light.

Be Thou my Wisdom, Thou my true Word;
I ever with Thee, Thou with me Lord.
Thou my great Father, I Thy dear son,
Thou in me dwelling, I with Thee one.

Be Thou my breastplate, my sword for the fight;
Be Thou my whole armour, be Thou my true might;
Be Thou my soul's shelter, be Thou my strong tower:
O raise Thou me heavenward, great Power of my power.

Riches I heed not, nor man's empty praise:
Be Thou mine inheritance now and always;
Be Thou and Thou only the first in my heart;
O Sovereign of heaven, my treasure Thou art.

High King of heaven, Thou heaven's bright Sun,
O grant me its joys after vict'ry is won;
Great Heart of mine own heart, whatever befall,
Still be Thou my vision, O Ruler of all.

(Ancient Irish)

CHRIST WITH US

My dearest Lord,
Be Thou a bright flame before me,
Be Thou a guiding star above me,
Be Thou a smooth path beneath me,
Be Thou a kindly shepherd behind me,
Today and evermore.

(St Columba)

CHRIST IN OTHERS

Christ the lowly and meek,
Christ the all powerful,
Be in the heart of each to whom I speak,
In the mouth of each who speaks to me,
In all who draw near me,
Or see me, or hear me!

(St Patrick)

THE POWER OF GOD

May the strength of God pilot us,
May the power of God preserve us,
May the wisdom of God instruct us,
May the hand of God protect us,
May the way of God direct us,
May the shield of God defend us,
May the host of God guard us
against snares of evil
and the temptations of the world.

(St Patrick)

THE PATH I WALK

The path I walk, Christ walks it.

May the land in which I am in be without sorrow.

May the Trinity protect me wherever I stay, Father, Son and
Holy Spirit.

Bright angels walk with me – dear presence – in every dealing.

In every dealing I pray them that no one's poison may reach me.

The ninefold people of heaven of holy cloud, the tenth force of
the stout earth.

Favourable company, they come with me, so that the Lord may
not be angry with me.

May I arrive at every place, may I return home; may the way in
which I spend be a way without loss.

May every path before me be smooth, may woman and child
welcome me.

A truly good journey! Well does the fair Lord show us a course,
a path.

attributed to St Columba

(Davies and Bowie, 1995, p. 38)

THE PATH OF RIGHT

When the people of the Isles come out in the morning to their
tillage, to their fishing, to their farming, or any of their various
occupations anywhere, they say a short prayer called 'Ceum na
Corach', 'The Path of Right', 'The Just or True Way'. If the
people feel secure from being overseen or overheard they croon,
or sing, or intone their morning prayer in a pleasing musical
manner. If, however, any person, and especially if a stranger is
seen in the way, the people hum the prayer in an inaudible
undertone peculiar to themselves, like the soft murmur of the
everlasting murmuring sea, or like the far-distant eerie sighing of
the wind among trees, or like the muffled cadence of far-away
waters, rising and falling upon the fitful autumn wind.

My walk this day with God,
My walk this day with Christ,
My walk this day with Spirit,
The Threefold all-kindly:
Ho! ho! ho! the Threefold all-kindly

My shielding this day from ill,
My shielding this night from harm,
Ho! ho! both my soul and my body,
Be by Father, by Son, by Holy Spirit:
By Father, by Son, by Holy Spirit.

Be the Father shielding me,
Be the Son shielding me,
Be the Spirit shielding me,
As Three and as One:
Ho! ho! ho! as Three and as One.

(Carmichael, 1976, p. 49)

GOD GUIDE ME

God guide me with Thy wisdom,
God chastise me with Thy justice,
God help me with Thy mercy,
God protect me with Thy strength.

God fill me with Thy fullness,
God shield me with Thy shade,
God fill me with Thy grace,
For the sake of Thine Anointed Son.

Jesu Christ of the seed of David,
Visiting One of the Temple,
Sacrificial Lamb of the Garden,
Who died for me.

(Carmichael, 1983, p. 65)

THE PRESENCE

The Lord is my shepherd:
therefore can I lack nothing.

Yea, though I walk through the valley of the shadow of death,
  I will fear no evil:
for thou art with me; thy rod and thy staff comfort me.

Psalm 23.1, 4

THE THREE EVERYWHERE

The Three who are over my head,
The Three who are under my tread,
The Three who are over me here,
The Three who are over me there,
The Three who are in the earth near,
The Three who are up in the air,
The Three who in heaven do dwell,
The Three in the great ocean swell,
Pervading Three, O be with me.

(McLean, 1961, p. 361)

THOU MY SOUL'S HEALER

Thou, my soul's Healer,
Keep me at even,
Keep me at morning,
Keep me at noon,
On rough course faring,
Help and safeguard
My means this night.
I am tired, astray, and stumbling,
Shield Thou me from snare and sin.

(Carmichael, 1976, p. 85)

HOSPITALITY

O King of the stars!
Whether my house be dark or bright,
Never shall it be closed to any one,
Lest Christ close His house against me.

If there be a guest in your house
And you conceal aught from him
'Tis not the guest that will be without it,
But Jesus, Mary's Son.

(Meyer, 1928, p. 100)

THE THREE

The Three Who are over me,
The Three Who are below me,
The Three Who are above me here,
The Three Who are above me yonder;
The Three Who are in the earth,
The Three Who are in the air,
The Three Who are in the heaven,
The Three Who are in the great pouring sea.

(Carmichael, 1976, p. 93)

HYMN OF ST PATRICK

Christ with me, Christ before me, Christ behind me,
Christ in me, Christ beneath me, Christ above me,
Christ on my right, Christ on my left,
Christ when I lie down, Christ when I sit down,
Christ when I arise,
Christ in the heart of every man who thinks of me,
Christ in the mouth of every one who speaks of me,
Christ in every eye that sees me,
Christ in every ear that hears me.

I arise today
Through a mighty strength,
The invocation of the Trinity,
Through belief in the threeness,
Through confession of the oneness
Of the Creator of Creation.

(Meyer, 1928, p. 27)

PRAISE GOD

Praise the Lord, ye servants:
O praise the Name of the Lord.
Blessed be the Name of the Lord:
from this time forth for evermore.
The Lord's Name is praised:
from the rising up of the sun unto the going down of the same.

Psalm 113.1–3

HAIL TO THE KING

Hail to the King, hail to the King,
Blessed is He, blessed is He,
Hail to the King, hail to the King,
Blessed is He who has come betimes,
Hail to the King, hail to the King,
Blessed be the house and all therein,
Hail to the King, hail to the King,
'Twixt stock and stone and stave,
Hail to the King, hail to the King,
Consign it to God from corslet to cover,
Be health of men therein,
Hail to the King, hail to the King,
Blessed is He, blessed is He,
Hail to the King, hail to the King,
Blessed is He, blessed is He,
Lasting round the house be ye,
Hail to the King, hail to the King,
Healthy round the hearth be ye,
Hail to the King, hail to the King,
Many be the stakes in the house
And men dwelling on the foundation,
Hail to the King, hail to the King,
Blessed is He, blessed is He,
Hail to the King, hail to the King,
Blessed is He, blessed is He.
Hail to the King, hail to the King,
This night is the eve of the great Nativity
Hail to the King, hail to the King,
Blessed is He, blessed is He,
Hail to the King, hail to the King,
Born is the Son of Mary the Virgin,
Hail to the King, hail to the King,
Blessed is He, blessed is He,
Hail to the King, hail to the King,
The soles of His feet have reached the earth,
Hail to the King, hail to the King,

Blessed is He, blessed is He,
Hail to the King, hail to the King,
Illumined the sun the mountains high,
Hail to the King, hail to the King,
Blessed is He, blessed is He,
Shone the earth, shone the land,
Hail to the King, hail to the King,
Blessed is He, blessed is He,
Hail to the King, hail to the King,
Heard the wave upon the strand,
Hail to the King, hail to the King,
Blessed is He, blessed is He,
Blessed is He, blessed is He,
Hail to the King, hail to the King,
Blessed the King,
Without beginning, without end,
To everlasting, to eternity,
To all ages, to all time.

(Carmichael, 1983, pp. 127–9)

CHRISTMAS CAROL

Hail King! hail King! blessed is He! blessed is He!
Hail King! hail King! blessed is He! blessed is He!
Hail King! hail King! blessed is He! the King, of whom we sing,
All hail! let there be joy!

This night is the eve of the great Nativity,
Born is the Son of Mary the Virgin,
The soles of His feet have reached the earth,
The Son of glory down from on high,
Heaven and earth glowed to Him,
All hail! let there be joy!

The peace of earth to Him, the joy of heaven to Him,
Behold His feet have reached the world;
The homage of a King be His, the welcome of a Lamb be His,
King all victorious, Lamb all glorious,
Earth and ocean illumed to Him,
All hail! let there be joy!

The mountains glowed to Him, the plains glowed to Him,
The voice of the waves with the song of the strand,
Announcing to us that Christ is born,
Son of the King of kings from the land of salvation;
Shone the sun on mountains high to Him,
All hail! let there be joy!

Shone to Him the earth and sphere together,
God the Lord has opened a Door;
Son of Mary Virgin, hasten Thou to help me,
Thou Christ of hope, Thou Door of joy,
Golden Sun of hill and mountain,
All hail! let there be joy!

(Carmichael, 1983, p. 133)

BLESSINGS

The Lord shall preserve thee from all evil:
yea, it is even he that shall keep thy soul.
The Lord shall preserve thy going out, and thy coming in:
from this time forth for evermore.

Psalm 121.7–8

BLESSING

May God the Father bless us;
May Christ take care of us;
May the Holy Spirit enlighten us
all the days of our life.
The Lord be our Defender
and Keeper of body and soul,
both now and forever,
to the ages of ages.

> (*Book of Cerne*, tenth century)

ST PATRICK'S BLESSING ON MUNSTER

Blessing from the Lord on High
Over Munster fall and lie;
To her sons and daughters all
Choicest blessing still befall;
Fruitful blessing on the soil
That supports her faithful toil.

Blessing full of ruddy health,
Blessing full of every wealth
That her borders furnish forth,
East and west and south and north;
Blessing from the Lord on High
Over Munster fall and lie!

Blessing on her peaks in air,
Blessing on her flagstones bare,
Blessings from her ridges flow
To her grassy glens below!
Blessing from the Lord on High
Over Munster fall and lie!

As the sands upon her shore
Underneath her ships, for store,
Be her hearths, a twinkling host,
Over mountain, plain and coast;
Blessing from the Lord on High
Over Munster fall and lie!

(Graves, 1917, p. 12)

THE BLESSING OF THE NEW YEAR

God, bless to me the new day,
Never vouchsafed to me before;
It is to bless Thine own presence
Thou hast given me this time, O God.

Bless Thou to me mine eye,
May mine eye bless all it sees;
I will bless my neighbour,
May my neighbour bless me.

God, give me a clean heart,
Let me not from sight of Thine eye;
Bless to me my children and my wife,
And bless to me my means and my cattle.
                    (Carmichael, 1983, p. 159)

SEA PRAYER

Helmsman: Blest be the boat.

Crew: God the Father bless her.

Helmsman: Blest be the boat.

Crew: God the Son bless her.

Helmsman: Blest be the boat.

Crew: God the Spirit bless her.

All: God the Father,
God the Son,
God the Spirit,
Bless the boat.

Helmsman: What can befall you
And God the Father with you?

Crew: No harm can befall us.

Helmsman: What can befall you
And God the Son with you?

Crew: No harm can befall us.

Helmsman: What can befall you
And God the Spirit with you?

Crew: No harm can befall us.

All: God the Father,
God the Son,
God the Spirit,
With us eternally.

Helmsman:	What can cause you anxiety And the God of the elements over you?
Crew:	No anxiety can be ours.
Helmsman:	What can cause you anxiety And the King of the elements over you?
Crew:	No anxiety can be ours.
Helmsman:	What can cause you anxiety And the Spirit of the elements over you?
Crew:	No anxiety can be ours.
All:	The God of the elements, The King of the elements, The Spirit of the elements, Close over us, Ever eternally.

(Carmichael, 1983, p. 333)

THE JOURNEYING BLESSING

Bless to me, O God,
The earth beneath my foot,
Bless to me, O God,
The path whereon I go;
Bless to me, O God,
The thing of my desire;
Thou Evermore of evermore,
Bless Thou to me my rest.

Bless to me the thing
Whereon is set my mind,
Bless to me the thing
Whereon is set my love;
Bless to me the thing
Whereon is set my hope;
O Thou King of kings,
Bless Thou to me mine eye!

(Carmichael, 1976, p. 181)

THOU GREAT GOD

Thou great God, grant me Thy light,
Thou great God, grant me Thy grace,
Thou great God, grant me Thy joy,
And let me be made pure in the well of Thy health.

Lift Thou from me, O God, my anguish,
Lift Thou from me, O God, my abhorrence,
Lift Thou from me, O God, all empty pride,
And lighten my soul in the light of Thy love.

As I put off from me my raiment,
Grant me to put off my struggling;
As the haze rises from the crest of the mountains,
Raise Thou my soul from the vapour of death.

Jesu Christ, O Son of Mary,
Jesu Christ, O Paschal Son,
Shield my body in the shielding of Thy mantle,
And make pure my soul in the purifying of Thy grace.

(Carmichael, 1976, p. 345)

DEATH PRAYER

O God, give me of Thy wisdom,
O God, give me of Thy mercy,
O God, give me of Thy fullness,
And of Thy guidance in face of every strait.

O God, give me of Thy holiness,
O God, give me of Thy shielding,
O God, give me of Thy surrounding,
And of Thy peace in the knot of my death.

Oh give me of Thy surrounding,
And of Thy peace at the hour of my death!

(Carmichael, 1976, p. 375)

JOYOUS DEATH

Give us, O God, the needs of the body,
Give us, O God, the needs of the soul;
Give us, O God, the healing balsam of the body,
Give us, O God, the healing balsam of the soul.

Give us, O God, the joy of repentance,
Give us, O God, the joy of forgiveness,
Wash Thou from us the lees of corruption,
Cleanse Thou from us the stain of uncleanness.

O great God, Who art on the throne,
Give to us the true repentance,
Give to us the forgiveness of sin –
Sin inborn and actual sin.

Give to us, O God, strong love,
And that beautiful crown of the King;
Give us, O God, the home of salvation
Within the beauteous gates of Thy kingdom.

May Michael, bright warrior of the angels,
Be keeping the evil enemies down;
May Jesus Christ the Son of David
Be giving us hospitality in the brightness of peace.
                    (Carmichael, 1976, p. 387)

BLESSINGS

The eye of the great God be upon you,
The eye of the God of glory be on you,
The eye of the Son of Mary Virgin be on you,
The eye of the Spirit mild be on you,
To aid you and to shepherd you;
Oh the kindly eye of the Three be on you,
To aid you and to shepherd you.

May the everlasting Father Himself take you
In His own generous clasp,
In His own generous arm.
May God shield you on every steep,
May Christ keep you in every path,
May the Spirit bathe you in every pass.

May God make safe to you each steep,
May God make open to you each pass,
May God make clear to you each road,
And May He take you in the clasp of His own two hands.

God's peace be to you,
Jesus' peace be to you,
Spirit's peace be to you
And to your children,
Oh to you and to your children,
Each day and night
Of your portion in the world.

The guarding of the God of life be on you,
The guarding of loving Christ be on you,
The guarding of the Holy Spirit be on you
Every night of your lives,
To aid you and enfold you
Each day and night of your lives.

(Carmichael, 1976, pp. 201–7)

PEACE

Peace between neighbours,
Peace between kindred,
Peace between lovers,
In the love of the King of life.

Peace between person and person,
Peace between wife and husband,
Peace between woman and children,
The peace of Christ above all peace.

Bless, O Christ, my face,
Let my face bless every thing;
Bless, O Christ, mine eye,
Let mine eye bless all it sees.
                    (Carmichael, 1976, p. 267)

TO BE WITH GOD

Almighty God,
Father, Son, and Holy Ghost,
to me the least of saints,
to me allow that I may keep a door in Paradise.
That I may keep even the smallest door,
the farthest, darkest, coldest door,
the door that is least used, the stiffest door.
If only it be in Thine house, O God,
that I can see Thy glory even afar,
and hear Thy voice,
and know that I am with Thee, O God.

(St Columba)

PRAYER TO THE TRINITY

Teach me O Trinity,
All men sing praise to Thee;
Let me not backward be,
Teach me O Trinity.

Come Thou and dwell within me,
Lord of the holy race;
Make here Thy resting-place,
Hear me O Trinity.

That I Thy love may prove,
Teach Thou my heart and hand,
Even at Thy command
Swiftly to move.

Like a rotting tree,
Is this vile heart of me;
Let me Thy healing see,
Help me O Trinity.

                    (Hull, 1913, pp. 157–8)

PRAISE TO THE TRINITY

I praise the threefold
Trinity as God,
Who is one and three,
A single power in unity,
His attributes a single mystery,
One God to praise.
Great King, I praise you,
Great your glory.
Your praise is true;
I am the one who praises you.
Poetry's welfare
Is in Elohim's care.
Hail to you, O Christ,
Father, Son
And Holy Ghost,
Our Adonai.

I praise two,
Who is one and two,
Who is truly three,
To doubt him is not easy,
Who made fruit and flowing water
And all variety,
God is his name as two,
Godly his words,
God is his name as three,
Godly his power,
God is his name as one,
The God of Paul and Anthony.

I praise the one,
Who is two and one,
Who is three together,
Who is God himself,
He made Mars and Luna.
Man and woman,

The difference in sound between
Shallow water and the deep.
He made hot and cold,
The sun and the moon,
The word in the tablet,
And the flame in the taper,
Love in our senses,
A girl, dear and tender,
And burned five cities
Because of false union.

(Davies and Bowie, 1995, p. 30)

PRAISE TO GOD

In the name of the Lord, mine to praise, of great praise,
I shall praise God, great the triumph of his love,
God who defends us, God who made us, God who saved us,
God our hope, perfect and honourable, beautiful his blessing.
We are in God's power, God above, Trinity's king.
God proved himself our liberation by his suffering,
God came to be imprisoned in humility.
Wise Lord, who will free us by Judgement Day,
Who will lead us to the feast through his mercy and sanctity
In Paradise, in pure release from the burden of sin,
Who will bring us salvation through penance and the five
    wounds.
Terrible grief, God defended us when he took on flesh.
Man would be lost if the perfect rite had not redeemed him.
Through the cross, blood-stained, came salvation to the world.
Christ, strong shepherd, his honour shall not fail.

(Davies and Bowie, 1995, p. 32)

DOXOLOGY

O praise God in his holiness:
praise him in the firmament of his power.

Let every thing that hath breath:
praise the Lord.

Psalm 150.1, 6

As it was, as it is, and as it shall be
Evermore, God of Grace, God in Trinity!
With the ebb, with the flow, ever it is so,
God of grace, O Trinity, with the ebb and flow.

References, Acknowledgements and Sources

The Psalms are from The Book of Common Prayer, the rights in which are vested in the Crown, and are reproduced by permission of the Crown's Patentee, Cambridge University Press.

Bede, trans. Leo Sherley-Price, 1956, *A History of the English Church and People*, Penguin.

Carmichael, A., 1983 (Vol. 1), 1976 (Vol. 3), *Carmina Gadelica*, Scottish Academic Press.

Clancy, T. O. and Márkus, G. (eds), 1995, *Iona: The Earliest Poetry of a Celtic Monastery*, Edinburgh University Press.

Davies, O. and Bowie, F., 1995, *Celtic Christian Spirituality*, SPCK.

Graves, Alfred, P., 1917, *A Celtic Psaltery*, SPCK.

Hull, Eleanor, 1913, *The Poem-Book of the Gael*, Chatto and Windus.

McLean, G. R. D., 1961, *Poems of the Western Highlanders*, SPCK.

Meyer, Kuno (trans.), 1928, *Selections from Ancient Irish Poetry*, Constable & Co.

Ó Fiaich, Tomás. 1974, *Columbanus: In His Own Words*, Veritas.

Williams, Ifor, 1972, *The Beginnings of Welsh Poetry*, University of Wales Press.

The Society for Promoting Christian Knowledge (SPCK) was founded in 1698. Its mission statement is:

To promote Christian knowledge by

- **Communicating the Christian faith in its rich diversity**

- **Helping people to understand the Christian faith and to develop their personal faith; and**

- **Equipping Christians for mission and ministry**

SPCK Worldwide serves the Church through Christian literature and communication projects in 100 countries, and provides books for those training for ministry in many parts of the developing world. This worldwide service depends upon the generosity of others and all gifts are spent wholly on ministry programmes, without deductions.

SPCK Bookshops support the life of the Christian community by making available a full range of Christian literature and other resources, providing support for those training for ministry, and assisting bookstalls and book agents throughout the UK.

SPCK Publishing produces Christian books and resources, covering a wide range of inspirational, pastoral, practical and academic subjects. Authors are drawn from many different Christian traditions, and publications aim to meet the needs of a wide variety of readers in the UK and throughout the world.

The Society does not necessarily endorse the individual views contained in its publications, but hopes they stimulate readers to think about and further develop their Christian faith.

For information about the Society, visit our website at
www.spck.org.uk, or write to:
SPCK, Holy Trinity Church, Marylebone Road,
London NW1 4DU, United Kingdom.